There's a M~~onster~~ Under ~~Over~~ My Bed!

Anita Khuttan

© 2021 Anita Khuttan. All rights reserved.

No part of this book may be reproduced, stored in a retrieval system, or transmitted by any means without the written permission of the author.

AuthorHouse™
1663 Liberty Drive
Bloomington, IN 47403
www.authorhouse.com
Phone: 833-262-8899

Because of the dynamic nature of the Internet, any web addresses or links contained in this book may have changed since publication and may no longer be valid. The views expressed in this work are solely those of the author and do not necessarily reflect the views of the publisher, and the publisher hereby disclaims any responsibility for them.

This book is printed on acid-free paper.

ISBN: 978-1-6655-2570-1 (sc)
ISBN: 978-1-6655-2571-8 (e)

Library of Congress Control Number: 2021909922

Print information available on the last page.

Published by AuthorHouse 05/25/2021

authorHOUSE®

"He's not here right now,

he comes out at night,

I hear him breathing, it gives me a fright".

"He's not here right now,

he shows up in the day,

he scares me to death, I can't even play".

"It's nothing I tell you", says mum whilst we wash.

"It's noise from outside, don't worry just hush".

"It's nothing I tell you, its noise from the house,

it's probably nothing but a sneaky mouse".

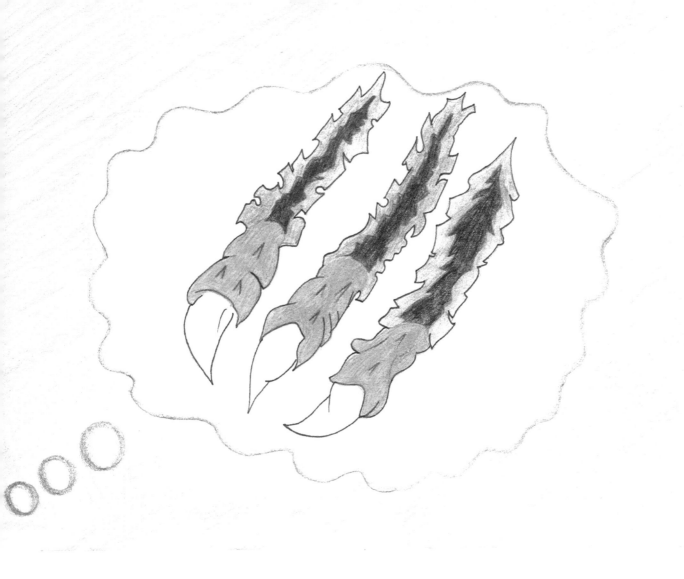

"But I've heard him scratching his claws on the floor,

I'm too scared to get up and run for the door".

"But I've seen his toes lower down to the ground,

I sink myself in further so I can't be found".

"What does he look like? He might not be scary".

"He is, he's loud, he roars, and his paws are hairy.

"What does he look like? He might be friendly".

"No! he's sneaky and giggly and his legs are spindly".

"Maybe today just wait till it's night,

if you face your fears, it might be alright".

"Maybe tonight get into your bed,

when you hear him above you, slowly raise your head.

You might surprise him and catch him off guard,

come on dear, being brave is not so hard".

It got dark and silent; the night drew nearer...

"I heard a shuffle coming from under the bed,

so, I gently lowered and tipped my head".

"I saw a head slowly appear from above,

he wasn't evil, he didn't hit nor shove".

"You're the monster under my bed?"

"And you're the monster who hovers overhead?"

"I'm not a monster".

"Nor I", he said.

"To think of the times, I've heard you and fled".

They both chuckled and laughed and giggled away...

until their eyes grew sleepy and they called it a day.

Next time you worry, when you hear a noise,

is it a monster playing with your toys?

About the Author

Anita Khuttan was born May 12, 1986, in Birmingham, West Midlands, United Kingdom. She spent most of her childhood being shy, secretive, and quiet and often created unusual explanations for things she didn't understand. She enjoyed reading and often imagined herself as the main character, going on adventures, solving mysteries, and getting herself entangled in thrilling situations. Anita Khuttan is a teacher by profession and has been teaching for 12 years.

Lightning Source UK Ltd.
Milton Keynes UK
UKHW050655101022
410222UK00008B/57

Have you ever been scared of falling asleep because you fear there's a monster that could be hiding under you bed?

In this story a little boy has those exact fears and while he wants to face the monster, he is also scared of what might happen to him if he does.

On the other hand, monsters may feel that humans are the scary ones and monster-like. After you read this story, you decide if the monster is under or over your bed.

author┐HOUSE®

ISBN 978-1-6655-2570-1
51699

9 781665 525701